Daughters of Narcissistic Mothers

A 5-Step Plan for New Moms to Break the Cycle and Raise Emotionally Secure Kids

mf

Disclaimer

By reading this guide, you are accepting the terms of this disclaimer in full. If you do not agree with these terms, please do not read or use this guide.

All content within this guide is provided for informational and educational purposes only and should not be considered medical, psychological, or other professional advice. The author is not a doctor, physician, psychologist, psychotherapist, counselor, or licensed healthcare provider. Reading or using this guide does not establish any form of a patient-client or therapeutic relationship.

Always consult with a physician, licensed therapist, or other qualified health professional regarding any questions or concerns you may have about your physical or mental health. Never disregard professional advice or delay seeking it because of something you have read in this guide.

The information presented in this guide is based on general research, personal interpretation, and publicly available sources. While reasonable efforts have been made to provide accurate and current information, the author and publisher make no representations or warranties about the completeness, accuracy, reliability, or suitability of the content. The author and publisher shall not be held liable for any errors, omissions, or outcomes related to the use of this guide.

You acknowledge that you are solely responsible for how you choose to use the information in this guide and that any actions you take based on this content are undertaken at your own risk. The publisher shall not be liable for any loss, injury, or damages arising from the application of any information provided herein.

This guide does not promise or guarantee any specific result, outcome, or improvement in well-being, mental health, or nervous system regulation. Individual results may vary.

Where applicable, any tools, concepts, or names mentioned are the property of their respective owners and are used strictly for identification or illustrative purposes. Their mention does not imply endorsement. Any individuals shown in the cover or promotional images are stock photography models, and image rights have been obtained through appropriate licensing agreements.

Table of Contents

Introduction

Motherhood is a journey filled with moments of joy, self-discovery, and—at times—waves of uncertainty. This uncertainty can feel even more intense if your own childhood was shaped by a parent whose needs consistently overshadowed your own. For those who grew up with a narcissistic mother, raising a child may feel like navigating uncharted territory, with an overwhelming desire to provide the love and stability you once longed for.

Parenting is challenging for all, but growing up with a narcissistic mother can leave behind emotional layers that are harder to navigate. You might find yourself dealing with unhealed wounds, overwhelming reactions, or automatic behaviors rooted in your early experiences.

These patterns can show up in your parenting—perhaps in the way you respond to your child or in the pressure you feel to meet unrealistic expectations. If this sounds familiar, it's important to understand that you're not alone, and that meaningful healing and change are both possible and achievable.

In this guide, we will talk about the following:

- Recognizing how the legacy of narcissistic parenting might influence your own approach to motherhood.
- Practical strategies to foster emotional safety for both yourself and your child.
- Tools to reparent your inner child while navigating the day-to-day realities of raising a family.
- Tips for modeling healthy relationships, setting boundaries, and cultivating a nurturing environment.

Breaking the cycle of narcissistic parenting isn't easy, but it's one of the most transformative gifts you can give to yourself and your child. With awareness, intention, and self-compassion, you can chart a new path—one grounded in love, connection, and security.

By the end of this guide, you'll have not only a deeper understanding of how to break free from toxic generational patterns but also actionable steps to create a healthier, more empowering approach to parenting. You have the ability to change the story—for yourself and your child.

Recognizing the Legacy

Growing up with a narcissistic mother can deeply impact your self-esteem and shape the way you approach parenting. This chapter delves into the defining traits, emotional scars, and learned behaviors that may still affect you today.

By recognizing these patterns, you can start the healing process and make intentional choices that lead to a healthier, more positive future. Understanding your past is a crucial step toward building a stable, nurturing environment for yourself and your child.

Traits of Narcissistic Mothers

Narcissistic mothers often have a strong need for admiration and control, which can manifest in various ways. Some common traits of narcissistic mothers include:

- ***Needs Always Come First***: Narcissistic mothers typically prioritize their own needs, desires, and emotions over their child's. This might mean moments where your achievements, feelings, or struggles were dismissed because they didn't align with her narrative or focus.

- ***Conditional Love***: Love is often tied to your performance. A narcissistic mother may have shown affection only when you met her expectations, leaving you feeling that being "good enough" came with strings attached.
- ***Excessive Control***: These mothers often attempt to dominate decisions in their children's lives, from minor choices to major ones, to maintain a sense of power. This control can stifle independence and leave you second-guessing yourself as an adult.
- ***Undermining Self-Esteem***: Narcissistic mothers may criticize, belittle, or dismiss their children's talents, opinions, or feelings. This erodes self-worth, leaving scars and a sense of inadequacy.
- ***Lack of Empathy***: An inability or unwillingness to understand or value others' feelings is a hallmark trait. Emotional support may have been infrequent or absent altogether during your childhood, making your own emotions feel unimportant.
- ***Drama and Manipulation***: Often, these mothers thrive on creating drama or conflict. They might manipulate situations or people to draw attention to themselves or to assert control, regardless of how it affects others.
- ***Jealousy or Competition***: They may feel threatened by their own children's success or happiness. This can

manifest as putting you down, downplaying your accomplishments, or making your moments about them.

- ***Exaggerated Sense of Self***: Narcissistic mothers often carry a grandiose view of themselves. This might mean they seek constant validation and expect praise, sometimes at the expense of acknowledging anyone else's efforts or emotions.
- ***Playing the Victim***: When confronted, these mothers may shift blame or cast themselves as the victim to avoid accountability. This tactic can leave their children feeling guilty for voicing concerns or standing up for themselves.
- ***Rigid Expectations***: They may impose strict and unyielding standards for success, behavior, or appearance. Failure to meet these expectations can result in rejection, criticism, or punishments rooted in emotional withdrawal.

Noticing these traits can help you see how they have affected the way you think, feel, and respond. It's not about blaming anyone—it's about understanding what happened so you can make better choices as a parent.

Common Wounds Passed Down from Narcissistic Parents

Children of narcissistic parents can develop a range of emotional wounds that can impact their lives well into adulthood. Some common wounds include:

- ***Low Self-Worth***: Growing up, your mother's approval may have felt conditional, based on achievements or how well you met her expectations. Over time, this can lead to feelings of being "not good enough," making it hard to feel confident in yourself or your abilities.
- ***Fear of Rejection***: If your emotional needs were frequently dismissed, you might now fear that others will reject you if you show vulnerability. This fear can make it difficult to trust others or express genuine emotions.
- ***Perfectionism***: Many daughters of narcissistic mothers develop a belief that they must be perfect to avoid criticism or earn love. This can translate into putting immense pressure on yourself, especially when it comes to parenting or personal achievements.
- ***Overthinking and Doubting Yourself***: Narcissistic mothers often make their children question their own feelings or judgments. Gaslighting and constant criticism can make you second-guess every decision and feel unsure of your choices.

- ***Guilt and Self-Blame***: You may have been made to feel responsible for your mother's emotions, leaving you with a tendency to blame yourself in relationships or when things go wrong. This can create heavy guilt, even over things that aren't your fault.
- ***Difficulty Setting Boundaries***: A lack of respect for your privacy or needs growing up may leave you feeling like it's wrong to establish boundaries. You might struggle with saying "no" or prioritizing your own well-being.
- ***Anxiety Around Relationships***: If love felt unpredictable or earned rather than freely given, you might find yourself anxious about maintaining relationships. This could include overanalyzing interactions or fearing that people will leave.
- ***Struggle to Express Feelings***: If expressing emotions was unsafe or dismissed as a child, you may now find it hard to identify or communicate what you're feeling. This can make it tough to connect deeply with others, including your own children.
- ***People-Pleasing Tendencies***: Being raised to prioritize your mother's needs over your own may have taught you to constantly seek approval by putting others first. This can lead to burnout and make it harder to care for yourself.

These emotional wounds don't define who you are, but they can quietly shape how you see yourself and relate to others.

Becoming aware of them allows you to heal and make healthier choices—for yourself and your child.

Emotional Patterns You May Be Repeating

We all have emotional patterns that we may be repeating without even realizing it. These patterns can stem from our childhood experiences, past traumas, or societal pressures. Some common emotional patterns that parents may unknowingly pass on to their children are:

- ***Seeking Approval***: You might find yourself constantly seeking validation from others, whether it's about your parenting choices or other aspects of life. This stems from growing up in an environment where love and approval were conditional, making you question your intrinsic worth.
- ***People-Pleasing***: To avoid conflict or criticism, you might prioritize keeping others happy, even at the expense of your own needs. When applied in parenting, this can look like over-accommodating your child to avoid them feeling upset, which can undermine boundaries.
- ***Fear of Making Mistakes***: High levels of criticism in childhood could leave you with a deep fear of failure. You might find yourself overthinking or stressing about being the "perfect" parent, rather than accepting that mistakes are part of the learning process.

- ***Difficulty Setting Boundaries***: Growing up with a mother who disregarded your needs might leave you struggling to say "no" or establish healthy limits. As a parent, this can blur the line between meeting your child's needs and neglecting your own emotional well-being.
- ***Overcompensating with Control***: You might overcorrect by trying to control every aspect of your child's life, fearing that if you don't, they'll lack guidance or structure. While well-intentioned, this can stifle your child's autonomy and individuality.
- ***Avoiding Emotional Conflict***: Due to a childhood filled with tension or arguments, you may avoid addressing emotional issues altogether. This can lead to unresolved problems within your family that build up over time.
- ***Hypervigilance to Criticism***: Being overly sensitive to even constructive feedback may stem from a childhood of harsh judgment. This can make parenting feel like walking on eggshells, as you might interpret normal challenges as personal failures.
- ***Suppressing Your Own Needs***: You might unconsciously replicate the pattern of ignoring your own emotions and needs, focusing entirely on others. This can result in burnout, leaving you emotionally unavailable to your child.

- ***Projecting Fear Onto Your Child***: Childhood experiences might lead to projecting fears about rejection, failure, or unworthiness onto your child. This can create pressure that affects how your child views themselves.
- ***Difficulty Showing Vulnerability***: If displaying emotions was met with dismissal or ridicule during your upbringing, you might hesitate to be emotionally vulnerable with your child. This could create distance, preventing deeper emotional bonds.

These emotional patterns can affect how you act as a parent without you even realizing it. When you understand them, you can make better choices that help you and your child feel safer and more connected.

How It Impacts You as a New Mom

Being a new mom can bring a flood of emotions, especially when past experiences with a narcissistic parent linger in the background. Perfectionism, guilt, fear, and emotional triggers from childhood may surface, making your role feel even more challenging.

These struggles, while difficult, present a chance to break free from old patterns and build a parenting approach rooted in love and security. This chapter explores these challenges and offers steps to help you approach motherhood with confidence and self-compassion.

Perfectionism, Guilt, and Fear

As a new mom, you may feel an overwhelming pressure to be perfect in every aspect of parenting. This pressure often stems from a deep-rooted belief that mistakes define your worth or that you need to prove yourself as a capable parent.

You might feel like every decision you make—big or small—carries immense weight, and any misstep could have lasting consequences for your child. This constant striving for perfection can make parenting feel exhausting and overwhelming, as you set impossible standards for yourself that no one could realistically meet.

Perfectionism can also make it difficult to enjoy the journey of motherhood. Instead of celebrating small wins or cherishing everyday moments, you might find yourself focusing on what you didn't do or what could have been done better. This mindset can rob you of the joy and connection that come with parenting, leaving you feeling like you're always falling short, no matter how much effort you put in.

Closely tied to perfectionism is guilt. ***Guilt*** can creep in when you feel like you're not doing enough, when you make mistakes, or even when you take time for yourself. You might feel guilty for not being present every moment, for losing your patience, or for not meeting the unrealistic expectations you've set for yourself.

This guilt can become a heavy burden, making it hard to relax and fully engage with your child. It can also lead to a cycle of overcompensating, where you try to make up for perceived shortcomings by pushing yourself even harder, which only adds to your stress.

Fear is another powerful emotion that often accompanies perfectionism and guilt. You may find yourself constantly worrying about whether you're doing a good job as a parent. This fear can stem from a desire to avoid repeating the patterns of your own upbringing or from a lack of confidence in your ability to provide the love and care your child needs. Fear can make you second-guess your decisions, leaving you feeling unsure and anxious about even the smallest choices.

These feelings of fear can also create a cycle of self-doubt. You might question your instincts, worry about how others perceive your parenting, or feel like you're not measuring up to other moms. This self-doubt can make it harder to trust yourself and your ability to navigate the challenges of motherhood. Over time, it can erode your confidence and leave you feeling isolated and overwhelmed.

It's important to recognize that these feelings—perfectionism, guilt, and fear—are common, especially for mothers who grew up in environments where love and approval were conditional. Understanding where these emotions come from is the first step toward breaking free from their grip. When you recognize and work through these feelings, it becomes easier to release the unrealistic expectations you've held onto and instead concentrate on what really counts: nurturing a loving and supportive bond with your child.

Overcorrecting or Overcompensating

When you've experienced a difficult or emotionally painful childhood, it's natural to want to do everything differently for your own child. You may feel a strong determination to avoid repeating the mistakes your mother made, but this can sometimes lead to overcorrecting.

Overcorrecting means trying so hard to be the opposite of your own mother that you lose balance in your parenting approach. For instance, you might avoid setting boundaries because you fear being too controlling, or you might hesitate to discipline your child because you don't want them to feel criticized. While these actions come from a place of love and good intentions, they can unintentionally create challenges for both you and your child.

Overcorrecting can make it difficult to find a middle ground in parenting. Boundaries, structure, and guidance are essential for a child's emotional development, but the fear of being too strict or too much like your own mother might hold you back from providing these.

This can lead to a parenting style that is overly permissive, where your child may struggle to understand limits or develop a sense of responsibility. It's important to remember that being different from your mother doesn't mean avoiding all forms of discipline or structure—it means finding a balanced approach that supports your child's growth while respecting their individuality.

Overcompensating is another common response to a difficult childhood. This happens when you try to make up for the emotional wounds you experienced by giving too much to your child. You might pour all your energy into ensuring they feel loved, supported, and cared for, often at the expense of your own needs.

While this level of dedication comes from a place of deep love, it can lead to exhaustion and burnout. Parenting is a demanding role, and when you neglect your own well-being, it becomes harder to show up for your child in the way you want to.

Overcompensating can also create an imbalance in your relationship with your child. Sometimes, when we're always giving and doing things for our children, we might accidentally make it harder for them to grow their independence and learn how to handle challenges by themselves.

Children thrive when they have the opportunity to explore, make mistakes, and grow, but overcompensating can sometimes take away these opportunities in an effort to shield them from discomfort or hardship.

Both overcorrecting and overcompensating are rooted in a desire to protect your child and give them the love and care you may have missed in your own childhood. However, these approaches can make it harder to find a healthy, sustainable way to parent. The key is to recognize when these patterns are showing up and to remind yourself that balance is essential.

Parenting isn't about being perfect, and making mistakes is completely normal. When you focus on creating a relationship rooted in love, respect, and understanding, you nurture your child's growth while also honoring your own well-being.

Emotional Triggers from Your Own Childhood

Parenting can stir up emotional memories in ways you don't always expect. Certain situations with your child—like tantrums, defiance, or even just needing attention—can echo moments from your own upbringing.

These moments can take you back emotionally, reminding you of how you were treated, whether your emotions were dismissed, or if you felt unheard, unsupported, or shamed.

You might:

- Feel a wave of rejection when your child pulls away or says something hurtful.
- Feel irritated or uncomfortable when your child cries or expresses feelings you weren't allowed to share.
- Experience anxiety or sadness when your baby cries for a long time, bringing up memories of your own unmet needs as a child.

These emotional reactions are not random—they're clues. They reveal areas that still feel tender, areas where your inner child might still be waiting for comfort, understanding, or acknowledgment. Recognizing these reactions helps you see that you're not overreacting—you're responding to deeper, unresolved pain.

When these moments happen, pause and breathe. Remind yourself that you're not in the past anymore. Ask gently, "What's really coming up for me right now? Is this emotion about today—or something I haven't had the chance to heal yet?"

This kind of reflection doesn't erase the trigger, but it helps soften your reaction. Instead of acting from a place of pain, you give yourself space to choose a calmer, more thoughtful response. The more often you do this, the more you build emotional strength—and the more trust you build with your child. These everyday moments of awareness can become small steps toward meaningful growth and stronger connection.

The 5-Step Cycle-Breaking Framework

In order to break the cycle of intergenerational trauma, it is important to have a framework that guides your actions and reactions in parenting. In this chapter, we will discuss the 5-step cycle-breaking framework, a practical tool that can help you navigate through difficult situations and be more intentional in your parenting.

Step 1: Awareness and Reflection

The first step to breaking the cycle of dysfunction is building awareness. Without it, you might unknowingly repeat harmful patterns from your own childhood. These patterns often run deep; you didn't choose them, but they can still influence your thoughts, feelings, and parenting.

Start by slowing down and giving yourself space to reflect. ***Think about your childhood***: What messages did you receive about love, trust, emotions, or mistakes? Were you allowed to cry without being shamed? Were your achievements celebrated only when they benefited your parent's image?

Were you made to feel responsible for your mother's happiness?

These early messages shape your inner voice and your beliefs about parenting. You might now find yourself reacting in ways that surprise you—getting overly upset when your child cries, feeling panicked when they ignore you, or needing to control their behavior to feel safe. These aren't random reactions. They often point to unhealed wounds from your own experience.

Ask yourself reflective questions like:

- "What emotions were not safe to express in my home growing up?"
- "How did my mother respond when I made a mistake?"
- "What fears or anxieties do I have as a mom now—and where might they come from?"
- "Am I parenting from love and connection, or from fear and survival?"

Also pay attention to what triggers you. A trigger is often a sign that something old is being touched in the present moment. For example, if your child whines and you instantly feel overwhelmed or angry, ask yourself why. Did you grow up being told that your needs were annoying or too much? If so, your child's neediness might unknowingly remind you of that experience.

Awareness isn't about placing blame on your parents or yourself. It's about seeing your experiences clearly, with both compassion and curiosity. When you begin to understand the root of your reactions, you reclaim your power. You stop parenting out of habit and begin making intentional choices based on the kind of parent you truly want to be—not just what you were shown growing up.

This reflective process takes time, and it may feel uncomfortable. But the more you notice your thoughts and reactions, the more you'll begin to see the difference between what's yours and what was passed down to you. That clarity gives you the freedom to let go of what doesn't serve you and your child.

Step 2: Emotional Boundaries and Safety

Once you've started to recognize how your past affects your present, the next step is creating ***emotional boundaries***. Emotional boundaries are not about shutting people out. They are about knowing where you end and others begin. They help you protect your energy, your peace, and your emotional space—so that you can show up fully for yourself and your child.

If you grew up with a narcissistic mother, your boundaries may have been ignored, pushed, or punished. You may have been taught to meet other people's needs first, even if it hurt you. You might have learned that saying "no" meant being selfish or disrespectful. Because of this, setting boundaries now can feel scary or wrong—but it's neither.

Healthy boundaries begin with self-awareness. Start by asking:

- "What situations make me feel emotionally drained or unsafe?"
- "Where do I feel responsible for someone else's feelings?"
- "What do I need in order to feel calm, respected, or in control?"

Next, create boundaries that reflect your needs. These might include:

- Limiting contact with people who manipulate or guilt-trip you.
- Taking a break from emotionally charged conversations.
- Saying "no" to visits or favors that disrupt your peace or parenting goals.
- Not explaining your parenting choices to those who constantly criticize them.

At the same time, focus on building emotional safety for your child. Let them know that their feelings are okay—that they don't need to hide or change how they feel to be loved. You can say things like:

- "It's okay to be mad. I'm here."
- "You can cry. I'll stay with you."
- "Your feelings are important, and I want to understand."

Children thrive in environments where their emotions are accepted and respected. When you create that space for them, they grow up confident and emotionally aware. They also learn how to respect your feelings in return—because they see you modeling boundaries and self-respect in daily life.

Setting emotional boundaries also means protecting ***your own*** well-being. That includes learning how to pause before reacting, stepping away when you're triggered, and reminding yourself that you are not a child anymore—you're an adult now. You get to decide what's okay and what's not. You get to choose what kind of parent you want to be.

If a relative oversteps your parenting choices or triggers old pain, you are allowed to take space. You don't owe anyone access to your time, energy, or child just because they're family. Boundaries are not walls—they are filters that keep what's good in and what's harmful out.

Setting emotional boundaries and creating a safe space for both you and your child lays the groundwork for a home full of trust, respect, and stability. It also teaches your child a vital skill—how to protect their own peace while respecting the feelings of others.

Step 3: Reparenting Your Inner Child

Reparenting your inner child is about giving yourself the care, comfort, and safety that may have been missing during your childhood. If you grew up with a narcissistic mother, you may have learned to ignore your own needs, quiet your feelings, or stay small to avoid conflict.

Those early survival habits often carry over into adulthood, especially into parenting. Reparenting helps you gently unlearn those habits and meet your own emotional needs—often for the very first time.

It starts with noticing the younger parts of you that still feel hurt, scared, or unloved. These feelings can show up when you're tired, overwhelmed, or triggered by your child's behavior. Instead of pushing those feelings away, ***pause and ask yourself***:

"What does my younger self need right now?": Maybe you need reassurance. Maybe you need rest. Maybe you just need someone to say, ***"You're doing a good job."***

Treat yourself the way you would care for your child. Speak kindly to yourself. Offer comfort. Let yourself cry if you need to. ***Say things like***:

- "You're allowed to feel this way."
- "You're not alone anymore."

- "You are worthy of love, even when you make mistakes."

Over time, reparenting also means challenging old beliefs. You may have been told you were too sensitive, not good enough, or only lovable when you pleased others. Those messages are not true, and they don't have to define you anymore.

Start rewriting your inner script:

- *Replace* ***"I'm failing"*** with ***"I'm learning."***
- Replace ***"I'm too much"*** with ***"My feelings are valid."***
- Replace ***"I can't do this"*** with ***"I'm doing my best, and that's enough."***

As you begin to care for your inner child, something changes—you no longer rely on your child to fill the emotional gaps left by your past. The way you respond starts to feel calmer, more thoughtful. Rather than reacting from old wounds, you begin to show up with steadiness and confidence.

Reparenting takes time and patience. But with each small act—speaking to yourself with kindness, making space for your feelings, honoring your own limits—you begin to feel more emotionally grounded. This work isn't just for you. It's also a gift to your child. The more you care for yourself, the more present, trustworthy, and emotionally available you become as a parent.

Step 4: Practical Parenting Tools for Secure Attachment

Secure attachment is the emotional bond between you and your child that makes them feel safe, loved, and understood. It doesn't come from being perfect—it comes from being present, responsive, and emotionally available. When a child feels secure, they trust that you'll be there for them, even when things get hard. This trust becomes the foundation for their emotional and social development.

Here are some simple, practical tools to help you build secure attachment:

1. **Be Present**

   Your presence matters more than perfection. Put away distractions, make eye contact, and spend time truly engaging with your child. This could be during play, meals, bedtime, or even short conversations. When your child knows you're fully there, they feel important.

2. **Respond with Empathy**

   Children don't need their feelings "fixed." They need to feel seen and heard. When your child cries, gets upset, or feels scared, resist the urge to distract or silence them. Instead, say:

- "That sounds really hard."
- "It's okay to feel sad. I'm here."
- "You're allowed to be upset. Let's get through it together."

These responses teach your child that emotions are not dangerous or shameful—they are normal and manageable.

3. **Set Loving Boundaries**

Children feel safe when they know there are clear, predictable rules. Boundaries don't have to be strict or cold—they can be calm and respectful. Instead of yelling "Stop that!" try:

- "I need you to use gentle hands."
- "It's okay to be angry, but it's not okay to hurt others."
- "Let's find another way to solve this."

Boundaries teach children self-control, respect, and safety—without fear.

4. **Use Active Listening**

When your child talks, stop what you're doing and truly listen. Get on their level, make eye contact, and repeat back what you heard to show you understand. This helps them feel validated and strengthens your emotional connection.

5. **Stay Consistent and Patient**

   Children thrive on routine and predictability. They feel secure when they know what to expect and how you'll respond. Be patient with their emotions and behaviors—especially during challenging moments. Mistakes are opportunities for connection, not punishment.

6. **Repair After Conflict**

   No parent handles every situation perfectly. What matters most is how you reconnect afterward. Say:

   - "I'm sorry for how I acted earlier. I love you."
   - "Let's talk about what happened. Your feelings are important."

   Repair strengthens trust and teaches your child that even hard moments can be worked through with love.

These tools help you do more than just manage behavior—they support your child's sense of self-worth, security, and connection. Building a secure attachment doesn't mean being perfect. It simply means showing up, responding with care, and trying again when mistakes happen.

Step 5: Building a New Legacy

Breaking the cycle of emotional pain is hard, brave work—but it leads to something beautiful: a new legacy.

<u>This step is about looking ahead and asking:</u>

- ***"What kind of future do I want for my child?"***
- ***"What kind of family culture do I want to create?"***

Instead of repeating the patterns you inherited—like control, emotional neglect, or conditional love—you now get to build something new. You get to create a home where love is unconditional, where emotions are safe, and where mistakes lead to connection—not shame.

1. **Celebrate How Far You've Come**

   Every time you respond with kindness instead of criticism, hold space for your child's feelings, or apologize after a mistake—you are doing something different. That's progress. Take time to notice and honor it.

   <u>Write down the wins, no matter how small:</u>

   - "I stayed calm when I was frustrated."
   - "I listened instead of reacting."
   - "I comforted myself instead of repeating old patterns."

These small changes build over time and help create a more emotionally healthy and supportive environment for your family.

2. **Model the Values You Want to Pass On**

   Children learn more from what you show than what you say. Teach your child by:

   - Speaking kindly—even when setting boundaries.
   - Owning your mistakes and making things right.
   - Respecting others while honoring your own needs.
   - Taking care of your mental and emotional health.

   These everyday moments become your child's blueprint for relationships, self-worth, and emotional balance.

3. **Embrace Imperfection**

   You don't need to do everything right to break the cycle. You just need to stay committed to growing. Teach your child that it's okay to mess up, to feel deeply, to start over. Show them that love doesn't disappear when things get hard.

   When you embrace your imperfections, you show your child it's okay to do the same. This helps them grow resilience, confidence, and kindness toward themselves—qualities that stay with them throughout life.

4. **Know That You Are the Turning Point**

   The work you're doing creates real change. It shapes how your child sees themselves, how they relate to others, and even how they'll raise their own children someday. You're not just ending a painful pattern—you're creating a new one. One built on emotional safety, trust, and genuine connection.

Your efforts are creating a lasting legacy that will impact future generations. Be proud of the foundation you're building—it's something your child will carry with them for a lifetime. And that is what truly makes it all worthwhile.

Healing While Parenting

Working through your past while raising a child can be tough, especially when both require your time and energy. Still, it's helpful to remember that caring for yourself and caring for your child don't have to compete—they can actually support each other and grow together.

When you take care of your own well-being, you show your child that it's okay to face challenges and take steps to feel better. Watching you work through hard moments teaches them that growth, self-care, and asking for support are all normal and healthy parts of life.

Can You Heal and Raise a Child at the Same Time?

Healing and parenting are not two separate paths—you can walk both at the same time. In fact, the experience of parenting often brings up the very wounds that need healing. The way your child looks to you for love, comfort, patience, and guidance may stir memories of what you didn't get growing up. These emotional echoes can feel confusing or painful, but they also serve a purpose: they reveal where care and attention are still needed within you.

Some moments in parenting will stretch you. A crying baby, a toddler's tantrum, or a child's emotional needs may feel overwhelming—not because you're doing something wrong, but because they touch parts of you that never felt soothed or seen. Instead of seeing these moments as signs of failure, try to view them as opportunities. These are not just challenges—they're openings to pause, notice your internal response, and choose a new one.

You don't have to be fully healed to be a good parent. No one is ever fully healed, and perfection is not the goal. What matters is your willingness to be present, to reflect on your actions, and to repair when things go off track. Children don't need perfect parents—they need real, connected ones. When you handle hard moments with honesty and care, you model emotional strength. You show your child that it's okay to have big feelings and that relationships can survive tough moments.

Parenting while working through your past may require making different choices than those you experienced growing up. It could involve setting boundaries, even when it feels difficult. It might mean allowing yourself to rest without guilt, reaching out for support, or letting go of the need to be perfect. It also includes learning to speak to yourself with compassion, especially when things don't go as planned.

Every time you respond with patience, every time you offer comfort—even when you're tired or triggered—you're not only helping your child feel secure, you're also rewriting the story for your younger self. That part of you that was once ignored or criticized finally gets to feel heard, loved, and safe through the care you now give to your child.

What makes personal growth during parenting so meaningful is the way it allows you and your child to develop together. As you support your child in understanding their feelings, expressing themselves, and feeling safe, you're also learning how to do that for yourself. This shared learning builds a deeper connection and helps create a more supportive and emotionally healthy family.

Self-Regulation Before Co-Regulation

To help your child feel safe and calm, the first step is to check in with yourself. This is called self-regulation. It means noticing what you're feeling—stress, anger, sadness, or overwhelm—and gently managing those emotions before responding to your child. When you are steady and composed, your child is more likely to feel secure, even during tense or emotional situations.

Think of yourself as your child's emotional anchor. If you appear anxious, reactive, or shut down, your child may mirror that behavior. But when you pause, take a breath, and respond calmly, you're teaching them that emotions don't have to control us. That's a lasting and valuable lesson.

This skill doesn't always come naturally—especially if your own emotions were dismissed or criticized growing up. If no one helped you learn how to regulate, it's understandable that you're still figuring it out now. The good news is that it's never too late to start.

Here are some simple tools to practice self-regulation:

- ***Breathe deeply and slowly***. Even three deep breaths can help reset your nervous system.
- ***Use kind self-talk***. Try saying things like, "This is hard, but I'm handling it," or "It's okay to feel this way."
- ***Take a short pause***. If your child is safe, step away for a moment to collect yourself.

If you lose your cool, don't get stuck in guilt. Repair the moment with honesty and love. You might say, "I got really frustrated and raised my voice. That wasn't fair to you. I'm sorry. I'm working on handling my big feelings better."

Moments like this teach your child that emotions are normal—and that it's possible to fix things with care and respect. When you model emotional awareness and repair, you give your child tools they'll carry with them for life.

What Progress Looks Like (It's Not Perfection)

Progress in parenting doesn't mean doing everything flawlessly. It means showing up with intention, noticing patterns, and choosing new ways of responding. Growth often looks quiet and slow. You may still face triggers, make mistakes, or feel overwhelmed—but how you respond is beginning to shift.

You'll know you're making progress when you:

- Pause before reacting, even just for a moment.
- Allow your child to express big emotions without shutting them down.
- Say "I'm sorry" after losing your temper.
- Use a gentler tone when speaking to yourself.
- Choose connection over control when things feel tense.

These moments might seem small at the time, but they add up to something meaningful—a family environment built on safety, trust, and love. Every act of patience, repair, or reflection helps create a more emotionally healthy space for your child.

Your child doesn't need perfection. They need presence. They need a parent who can admit mistakes, model emotional honesty, and keep coming back to the relationship with care.

That's how they learn to love themselves and others, even when life feels messy.

Parenting while healing is hard—but it makes a real difference. Every small step you take helps both you and your child grow. You're creating a home filled with honesty, care, and love. That's what truly helps break the cycle and build something better.

Breaking the Emotional Inheritance

Breaking free from patterns of emotional inheritance is one of the most meaningful gifts you can offer—to both your child and yourself. This chapter will explore how to model emotional intelligence, avoid shame-based parenting, and help your child feel that they are truly "good enough." These steps support a more secure and emotionally healthy environment, breaking harmful cycles that may have started in your own childhood.

How to Model Emotional Intelligence

Children learn about emotions by watching us. When you model emotional intelligence, you teach your child how to identify, express, and manage their feelings in healthy ways. Here's how to get started:

1. **Name and Validate Your Feelings**

   Instead of hiding your emotions, show your child how to name them. For example, if you're frustrated, you might say, "I feel frustrated because I spilled my coffee. I'm going to take a deep breath to calm down." This normalizes emotions and shows them how to handle difficult feelings.

2. **Practice Emotional Awareness**

   Pay attention to your own emotional state and reactions. For instance, if you notice yourself getting irritated, pause and ask yourself why. Children who see their parents reflecting on emotions learn to do the same.

3. **Stay Calm During Conflict**

   Use disagreements as opportunities to model respectful communication. For example, if you're upset, you can say, "I'm feeling frustrated, so I need a moment to think before we keep talking." This teaches them that it's okay to step away, process emotions, and return when you're ready.

4. **Apologize When Needed**

   If you lose your temper, owning it and apologizing shows emotional maturity. You might say, "I'm sorry for yelling. That wasn't the right way to handle things. I'll try to do better next time." This helps your child feel safe to make mistakes and repair relationships.

Showing your child what it looks like to handle emotions thoughtfully helps them build important life skills—like understanding themselves, caring about others, and staying steady through big feelings.

Preventing Shame-Based Parenting

Shame-based parenting communicates to children that they are inherently bad or unworthy. Breaking this cycle means replacing shame with understanding, patience, and love. Here's how:

1. **Focus on Behavior, Not the Child**

   When correcting your child, emphasize their actions instead of labeling them. For example, instead of saying, "You're so careless!" you can gently say, "That was a messy spill—how about we clean it up together?" This separates their behavior from their worth.

2. **Avoid Overreacting**

   Take a moment to respond calmly when your child makes a mistake. If you yell or harshly criticize, it can create deep feelings of shame. Instead, acknowledge what happened and guide them toward a solution. For instance, say, "Mistakes happen. What can we do better next time?"

3. **Build Their Sense of Worth**

   Remind your child that they are loved and valued, no matter what. Saying things like, "I love you even when you're upset" or "You're trying really hard, and I see that" reinforces their self-worth and keeps shame from taking root.

4. **Reflect on Your Own Responses**

   Think about where shaming responses might come from—was this how you were parented? Understanding your triggers can help you pause and make different choices when interacting with your child.

Breaking the habit of shame-based parenting takes practice, but every effort builds a stronger, healthier relationship with your child.

Teaching Your Child They Are "Good Enough"

Teaching your child that they are "good enough" is essential for their emotional security and confidence. Here's how you can foster this mindset:

1. **Celebrate Effort Over Perfection**

   Highlight your child's effort rather than focusing on the outcome. For example, say, "You worked so hard on this drawing!" instead of just, "What a perfect picture!" This shows them that trying matters more than being perfect.

2. **Encourage Self-Expression**

   Allow your child to explore their interests and make choices. Whether it's picking their own clothes or choosing an activity, giving them a voice builds confidence and self-trust.

3. **Create a Safe Environment for Mistakes**

   Teach your child that mistakes are learning opportunities, not failures. When they mess up, reassure them by saying, "It's okay to make mistakes. What can we learn from this?" This helps them feel secure in taking risks and trying new things.

4. **Use Affirmations and Encouragement**

   Offer positive reinforcement frequently. Simple phrases like, "You are so kind" or "I'm proud of you for trying" go a long way in building their belief that they are enough just as they are.

5. **Be Mindful of Comparisons**

   Avoid comparing your child to siblings, peers, or even yourself. Instead, focus on their unique strengths. For instance, say, "You're really great at solving puzzles!"

instead of, “Your brother solves them faster.” This helps them appreciate their own abilities without feeling the need to compete.

When you reinforce your child’s sense of being “good enough,” you help them grow into confident and emotionally secure individuals.

Changing deep emotional habits isn’t easy, but each small, loving effort makes a real difference. Sharing your feelings with care, staying patient, and helping your child feel seen and appreciated creates space for a healthier, more connected family life.

Remember, change doesn’t happen overnight, so treat yourself with kindness and recognize the little victories along the way. Each day, you’re creating a safer and more loving environment—not just for your child, but for yourself too.

Navigating Tricky Family Dynamics

Family relationships can be complicated, especially if you grew up with a narcissistic mother. When you become a mom yourself, these challenges can become even harder to handle. It's normal to want to protect your own child from the hurt you may have gone through, but figuring out how to do this while managing old wounds can feel overwhelming.

This chapter will walk you through real-life steps for setting healthy boundaries, keeping your child emotionally safe, and dealing with guilt or family expectations.

Setting Boundaries with Your Mother

Creating and standing by boundaries with a narcissistic mother can be tough, but it is important for your peace of mind and your child's well-being. Boundaries are rules you put in place to show what you're okay with and what you're not. When you set these limits, you are honoring your needs and teaching your child that their feelings and safety matter, too.

Why Boundaries Are Important

Without clear boundaries, your mother's wants or emotions can take over, leaving you stressed, drained, or guilty. Boundaries help you keep enough emotional energy to care for yourself and your child. They also show your child what healthy relationships look like—ones based on respect and kindness, not on fear or control.

How to Set Boundaries:

- ***Figure out your limits***: Think about what situations make you or your child feel upset, unsafe, or pressured. For example: Does your mother criticize your choices or ignore your rules for your child?
- ***Speak up***: Use direct but kind words to share your limits. You could say, "Please do not compare my child to others," or "I don't want to talk about my parenting decisions.
- ***Be consistent***: If your mother ignores your boundary, remind her each time. For instance, if she keeps bringing up something you asked her not to, gently repeat that you don't want to discuss it.
- ***Use consequences***: If repeating yourself isn't working, set a consequence. This could be ending a visit early, limiting phone calls, or only meeting in public places where you feel more in control.

- ***Protect your space***: You might decide that some topics or times are off-limits, like not accepting surprise visits or blocking calls during family time with your child.

Setting boundaries isn't always smooth. Your mother might ignore your limits, react angrily, or try to make you feel guilty. Stand firm. Explain that your choices are about protecting your family's health, not about punishing her. Over time, being steady with your boundaries shows your child that they can stand up for themselves, too.

Protecting Your Child from Emotional Harm

You may worry a lot about your child experiencing the same hurt you did. Being aware is the first step to making things better. Here's how you can help your child feel emotionally safe—especially around family:

Create a Safe Space

- ***Welcome feelings***: Show your child that all emotions are okay. Let them know it's fine to feel sad, angry, or afraid. For example, you might say, "It looks like you're upset. Do you want to talk or need a hug?"
- ***Predictable routines***: Make home a place where your child knows what to expect, like reading before bed or sharing meals together. Consistency helps children feel safe and know what is coming next.
- ***Kindness at home***: Use gentle words and actions. If you make a mistake, such as raising your voice,

apologize. This shows your child that everyone messes up but can fix things and stay connected.

Limit Harmful Interactions

- ***Supervise visits***: If you notice your mother talking down to your child or ignoring your rules, step in. You might choose to only allow visits when you are present or cut them short if negative behavior happens.
- ***State your rules***: Let your mother know which behaviors are not allowed around your child, like yelling, rude remarks, or pressure to keep secrets.
- ***Trust your instincts***: If something feels off during family gatherings, it's okay to leave or say no to future invitations.

Boost Emotional Skills

- ***Talk about feelings***: Help your child name emotions: "You look disappointed—did something not go your way?" Give simple ways to cope, like deep breaths or drawing their feelings.
- ***Encourage expression***: Praise your child when they speak up about their feelings. Let them know their voice matters, even if it's different from what others in the family might expect.

Protecting your child also means choosing yourself sometimes—stepping away from old patterns so you can be the parent you wish you'd had.

Dealing with Guilt and Cultural Pressure

Setting boundaries with your mother or limiting contact can bring up a lot of guilt or conflict—especially if your family or culture values obedience and staying close. You might hear things like, "She's your mother—you have to forgive her," or "Family is everything." These beliefs can make you doubt your decisions, even if you know they're best for your child.

Coping with Guilt

- ***Name your feelings***: Remind yourself that feeling guilty doesn't mean you're wrong. You are not selfish for keeping yourself and your child safe.
- ***Check your reasons***: Ask yourself, "Am I making this choice to protect my child and myself?" If the answer is yes, it is the right decision, even if others disagree.
- ***Rewrite old beliefs***: It's okay to change the rules about what family means to you and your child. Family should make you feel cared for and respected—not afraid or small.

Handling Cultural Pressure

- ***Lean on support***: Find others who understand what you're going through. This could be friends, a counselor, or a support group for parents breaking unhealthy patterns.

- ***Explain as needed***: If you must respond to family questions, keep it simple: "We're doing what feels best for our family right now."
- ***Trust your journey***: Remember, you are the parent now. Your main job is to give your child a healthy, loving start—even if it looks different from the way you were raised.

Letting go of old patterns can be difficult, and it's not unusual to face resistance from your mother or other relatives. That doesn't mean you're doing anything wrong. Every time you protect your well-being and your child's, you're creating a new kind of family legacy—one grounded in love, safety, and mutual respect.

When You Slip Up (and You Will)

Parenting is tough on its own, and even more so when you're still working through the pain of your own upbringing. For daughters of narcissistic mothers, there's often a deep desire to give your children what you never received—unconditional love, support, and emotional safety. But being a parent doesn't mean getting everything right. Mistakes are part of the process. What truly matters is how you handle those moments when they arise.

This chapter focuses on giving yourself grace, repairing after missteps, and talking openly with your kids when emotions run high. Mistakes don't define you as a parent—how you recover and grow does.

Grace Over Guilt

Mistakes can often bring a strong sense of guilt, especially when you're holding onto the emotional burden of your past. You might feel like every slip-up is proof that you're not succeeding as a mother. However, guilt doesn't serve you or your child. What truly makes a difference is grace, choosing to show yourself compassion and understanding.

What Does Grace Look Like?

Grace means recognizing that perfection isn't the goal. It allows you to understand that making mistakes and course-correcting are part of parenting and life. For example:

- You yelled because you were overwhelmed. Grace says, "I had a lot on my plate, and I reacted poorly—but I can make it right."
- You didn't handle your child's emotions well. Grace says, "I'm learning how to respond differently, and that takes time and practice."

Where guilt blames you, grace gives you permission to accept, grow, and move forward.

Practical Steps to Choose Grace Over Guilt

1. ***Pause and Reflect***: After a mistake, pause instead of spiraling into self-criticism. Ask yourself, "What triggered my reaction? What can I learn from this?"
2. ***Reframe the Narrative***: Shift from "I'm a terrible mom" to "I'm a mom who is learning." This small change helps create a healthier internal dialogue.
3. ***Separate Behavior from Identity***: You are not your mistakes. A single bad moment doesn't undo all the love and care you give every day.
4. ***Practice Self-Compassion***: Speak to yourself as kindly as you would a friend. Remind yourself, "I'm doing my best, and that's enough."

Choosing grace instead of guilt shows both you and your child that mistakes are a normal part of life and don't take away your value.

Scripts to Repair and Reconnect

Apologizing and making things right are important parts of parenting, even though many of us didn't grow up learning how to do them. If you were raised by a narcissistic mother, you may have been taught to hide mistakes or avoid showing vulnerability. But breaking the cycle means teaching your child a better way—by showing them how to handle conflict with honesty, care, and respect.

Why Repair Matters

Repair strengthens trust. It shows your child that even when things go wrong, relationships can be mended. It also teaches them that it's safe to make mistakes and that accountability is important. By reconnecting after a tense moment, you're creating an emotionally secure environment.

How to Apologize the Right Way

A good apology is:

- ***Sincere***: It's about your behavior, not your child's.
- ***Ownership-focused***: There's no shifting blame or deflecting responsibility.
- ***Empathetic***: It validates your child's experience and emotions.

Here are some examples of effective repair scripts for everyday situations:

1. ***After Losing Your Temper***

   "I'm sorry I shouted earlier. It wasn't okay for me to raise my voice, and I know it might have made you feel upset or afraid. I was feeling frustrated, but that's not your fault. Next time, I'll try to take a breath before responding."

2. ***After Dismissing Their Feelings***

   "When I said, 'It's not a big deal,' I see now that it made you feel unheard. I should have listened better. How do you feel about what happened?"

3. ***After Overreacting***

   "When I saw the spilled milk, I yelled, and that wasn't fair to you. I should have stayed calm. I'm sorry I made you feel bad, and I'd like to help you clean up together."

Apologies don't need to be long or perfect. What matters most is that they are genuine and followed by a change in behavior.

After apologizing, offer reassurance. Remind your child that mistakes don't define relationships. You can say something like, "Even when I mess up, I love you, and we're okay."

How to Talk to Your Kids After a Trigger

Sometimes, your child's behavior or a stressful situation can stir up old emotions or reactions from your own past. These moments can feel overwhelming, especially if they remind you of unresolved wounds or patterns from your childhood.

When this happens, it's essential to give yourself the space to reset before engaging with your child. Taking a pause allows you to approach the situation with patience, clarity, and intention.

1. **Pause and Reset**

   When you feel triggered, your first priority is to calm your own emotions. This might mean stepping away for a moment to breathe, grounding yourself, or simply taking a few seconds to collect your thoughts. You can say to your child, "I need a moment to calm down so I can talk to you better." This not only helps you regulate your emotions but also models healthy coping strategies for your child.

2. **Acknowledge What Happened**

   Once you're calm, start the conversation by acknowledging the situation and taking responsibility for your actions. For example, you might say:

- “I got upset earlier, and I wish I had handled it differently. I’m working on staying calmer next time.”
- “I raised my voice, and that wasn’t okay. I’m sorry for how I reacted.”

Taking responsibility for your actions teaches your child that it’s okay to make mistakes and that healing and connection are always possible.

3. **Invite Their Perspective**

After acknowledging your actions, invite your child to share their feelings about what happened. This helps them feel heard and valued. You can ask:

- “How did you feel when that happened?”
- “What was going through your mind earlier?”

These open-ended questions encourage your child to express themselves and show that their perspective matters. Be sure to listen without interrupting or defending your actions.

4. **Clarify That It’s Not Their Fault**

Children often internalize their parents’ emotions, believing they are to blame for outbursts or conflicts. It’s crucial to reassure your child that your reaction was not their fault. You might say:

- "When I got angry, it wasn't because of you. Sometimes grown-ups have big feelings too, and I'm learning how to handle mine."
- "You didn't do anything wrong. I was feeling overwhelmed, and I reacted poorly."

This helps your child understand that they are not responsible for managing your emotions, which is an important boundary to establish.

5. **Use Simple, Age-Appropriate Language**

When talking to your child, keep your words clear and age-appropriate. Younger children may need simpler explanations, while older kids might appreciate more detail. For example:

- For a toddler: "Mommy got upset, but it wasn't your fault. I love you, and I'm sorry."
- For an older child: "I was feeling stressed earlier, and I didn't handle it well. I'm working on doing better, and I appreciate your patience."

The aim is to speak in a way your child can truly understand—and that helps them feel safe, heard, and supported.

6. **Reassure and Reconnect**

End the conversation by reinforcing your love and commitment to your child. Let them know they are safe, loved, and that your relationship is strong. You might say:

- "Even when I make mistakes, I love you, and we're okay."
- "I'm here for you, and we'll figure things out together."

This kind of reassurance helps your child feel secure and teaches them that relationships can withstand challenges.

Having honest, open conversations after a triggering moment not only repairs the immediate situation but also builds long-term trust. It shows your child that it's okay to make mistakes as long as you take responsibility and work to make things right. Over time, these moments of repair teach your child valuable life skills, such as emotional regulation, empathy, and accountability.

Building a Village That Heals

Raising a child can be incredibly fulfilling, but it's not without its hard days—especially when you're unlearning old habits and figuring out new ways to parent. It's normal to feel stretched thin sometimes. You weren't meant to do this alone. Having the right people beside you—those who offer steady support, honest encouragement, and a safe place to land—can make all the difference for both you and your child.

This chapter explores how to build that village—from finding support, to surrounding yourself with healthy relationship examples, to reshaping motherhood in a way that aligns with your values and the kind of life you want to create.

Finding Support Through Therapy, Groups, and Friendships

Balancing the demands of parenting alongside your own personal challenges requires a strong support system—sometimes more than you might expect. It's easy to feel like you have to handle everything alone, but building genuine connections with others can bring much-needed stability. Those connections not only help you stay grounded but also foster a caring space where your child can truly flourish.

1. **Therapy as a Foundation**

   Therapy can be a priceless tool in your healing process. A good therapist can help you work through past trauma, build healthier coping mechanisms, and approach parenting with more confidence and calmness. Therapy also benefits the parent-child dynamic by promoting increased emotional awareness.

   If traditional therapy isn't an option due to time or cost constraints, consider group therapy sessions or free resources available in your community. Many therapists also offer sliding scale payments or online sessions, giving flexible options for busy parents.

2. **Parenting or Support Groups**

   Joining a parenting group connects you with others who know exactly what you're going through. These groups are more than a place to exchange tips—they're a lifeline for emotional support. Whether online or in person, parenting circles can foster understanding, offer advice, and affirm that you're not alone in your challenges.

   Some parents find solace in groups that focus on specific topics like parenting after trauma or single-parent communities. Explore what feels right for you.

3. **Friendships with Depth**

   Supportive friendships can make a big difference. Spend time with people who value honesty, show kindness, and support your growth. Look for connections with those who understand what you're working toward and who cheer you on—whether it's a big milestone or a small parenting win.

   Don't hesitate to set boundaries with relationships that feel draining or unsupportive. Your time and energy are valuable. Prioritize friendships that uplift and energize you.

Teaching Children About Healthy Relationships

Kids learn about relationships by watching the people around them. The way you interact with others shows them what love, respect, and connection really mean. When you're thoughtful about how you relate to people, you're giving your child a powerful example that will shape how they build their own relationships now and in the future.

1. **The Importance of Modeling**

   Children learn more from what they see you do than what they hear you say. If they observe you apologizing after a mistake, handling conflict with respect, or setting firm but kind boundaries, they internalize these behaviors as the norm. Your choices shape their understanding of what healthy relationships look like.

For example, if you treat yourself with kindness after a bad day, your child learns the value of self-compassion. Modeling this behavior teaches them how to nurture themselves emotionally.

2. **Encouraging Open Communication**

   A healthy relationship relies on open communication. Encourage your child to express their feelings and thoughts, and practice being an attentive, nonjudgmental listener. When your child feels safe to share with you, they carry that skill into relationships with peers, friends, and eventually, partners.

Even when it's challenging, validate their emotions and guide them to express themselves respectfully. This builds their confidence and strengthens your connection with them.

3. **Establishing Boundaries with Care**

   Boundaries teach children the importance of respect—both for themselves and others. Consistently reinforce healthy boundaries at home, whether it's about respecting personal space, managing screen time, or having age-appropriate responsibilities.

When your child sees you set and maintain boundaries in your own interpersonal relationships, they learn how boundaries provide safety and stability in healthy connections.

Redefining "Motherhood" on Your Own Terms

Choosing to break free from unhealthy patterns often means challenging the usual ideas about what being a mother "should" look like. Real motherhood isn't about meeting other people's expectations—it's about doing what feels right for you, what helps your child grow, and what keeps you well.

Release the Pressure of Perfection

Perfectionism is often a lasting effect of growing up with a narcissistic parent. But striving to be a perfect mother isn't realistic—or needed. Instead, aim to be a "good enough" mom who offers love, safety, and steady support. Embracing your imperfections lets you parent more authentically and with less guilt.

Prioritize Your Unique Strengths

Forget the comparison game. Your worth as a mother isn't measured by how closely you follow societal norms or other people's advice. Reflect on your own strengths, what brings you and your child joy, and how you can create a family culture that reflects your values.

Whether you're the arts-and-crafts kind of mom or the adventure-in-the-backyard type, leaning into your authentic style as a parent benefits both you and your child.

Build a Legacy of Emotional Safety

Motherhood, for you, may symbolize creating the childhood you never had. This involves making a conscious choice to parent in ways that prioritize emotional connection and security. Every time you choose understanding over criticism or patience over frustration, you're laying the foundation for a new kind of family legacy.

Creating a supportive village takes time—it's not something you build overnight. It's a continuous process of finding the right people, spaces, and resources that help lighten the load. With therapy, meaningful relationships, and a sense of community, you create more room to focus on what truly matters.

And as you model healthy connections and shape motherhood in a way that reflects your values, you're not just ending an old pattern—you're laying the foundation for a brighter future.

Moving Forward with Hope

Being a mom while carrying the weight of a tough past isn't easy. But even the smallest choices you make to do things differently can make a real difference—for you and your child. Growth doesn't happen overnight. It shows up in little wins, proud moments, and in creating the kind of home that feels safe, loving, and steady—the kind of childhood you may not have had, but are now giving.

This chapter will guide you in making meaningful progress, celebrating your parenting wins, and purposefully fostering a nurturing environment for your child..

Measuring Growth in Small Wins

Big changes rarely happen overnight. Real growth comes from small, steady steps. Learning to notice and celebrate those steps will keep you moving forward and help you see how far you've come.

1. **Look for Little Changes**

   Pay attention to the daily moments that show you're growing. Did you stay calm when your child had a meltdown? Did you take a deep breath before reacting to something stressful? These small changes matter. Each one shows that you're choosing a different path than the one you grew up with.

2. **Notice How You Feel**

   Your feelings can be a quiet reminder of the progress you've made. Maybe you stay calmer during tough moments, or notice that certain triggers don't affect you the way they used to. These small shifts may not seem big, but they're meaningful signs that you're growing and changing in the right direction.

3. **Reflect on Your Bond with Your Child**

   Ask yourself how your relationship with your child feels. Are they coming to you for comfort or help? Do they feel safe to express their feelings around you? If the answer is "yes," that's proof you're creating the secure, loving environment they need.

4. **Take Time to Celebrate**

   Each win, no matter how small, is worth celebrating. Write down one thing you're proud of each week, like handling a difficult situation with patience or giving your child space to be themselves. These notes can remind you that you're making progress, even when it doesn't feel obvious.

Raising a Child You Feel Proud Of

A proud parent isn't defined by perfection but by presence—by showing up, offering love, and creating a space where your child feels secure and seen. True pride grows in the small, consistent moments of connection and care.

1. **Focus on Love and Connection**

   What your child will remember most isn't whether their home was spotless or if you always got everything right. They'll remember the moments of love—reading a book together, laughing over a silly joke, or hugging after a long day. Make those moments a priority.

2. **Encourage Them to Be Themselves**

   Celebrate your child's unique personality and interests, even if they're different from what you imagined. This teaches them that they are enough just as they are, which is one of the most valuable lessons you can give them.

3. **Be a Role Model**

   What you do matters more than what you say. When you treat others with kindness, admit your mistakes, and show respect in everyday moments, your child learns by watching. These real-life examples shape their understanding far more than words alone ever could.

4. **Mistakes Are Learning Moments**

   You will make mistakes, and that's okay. When you do, show your child that it's normal to mess up. Say, "I'm sorry for raising my voice earlier. I was frustrated, but it wasn't okay." This helps them see that mistakes don't define you—a thoughtful response to them does.

Creating the Childhood You Never Had

For daughters of narcissistic mothers, becoming a parent opens the door to rewriting the story. Creating a home filled with love, safety, and trust gives your child what you may have missed and helps heal the parts of yourself that needed that same care.

1. **Create a Safe Emotional Space**

   Make your home a place where feelings are welcome. When your child is upset, listen to them and help name what they're feeling. Say, "I see you're angry. Do you want to talk about it?" This tells them it's okay to feel and that you're there to support them through it.

2. **Build Trust Through Consistency**

   Children thrive when they know what to expect. Stick to your promises and keep routines where you can. This creates a sense of safety that lets them flourish, and it models trust for them as they grow.

3. **Add Simple Joys**

   Create happy memories with small rituals. It could be regular picnics in the park, Sunday pancakes, or dancing in the kitchen. These simple, joyful moments become the foundation of their favorite childhood memories.

4. **Love Without Strings**

   One of the most important changes you can make is to show unconditional love. Your child should know they don't have to earn your affection—it's already theirs. Remind them often that you love them for who they are, not just for what they achieve.

5. **Heal as You Go**

   Building a childhood full of love and care for your child also helps you heal the wounds of your past. You might find comfort in the safety and joy you're creating, not just for them but for the part of yourself that longed for it, too.

> Moving forward with hope is about progress, not perfection. Each small win matters. Each moment of pride in your parenting builds confidence. Each choice to fill your child's world with love and security creates a cycle of kindness and strength.

The love and care you show your child are changing your story, too. Little by little, you're creating a life built on trust, closeness, and new beginnings. You and your child are growing something different—something better—one day at a time.

Conclusion

Breaking the cycle of emotional harm and raising a child with love and security is a big challenge. Choosing to face your past and parent with purpose shows how strong and caring you are. This guide is here to support you as you reflect, grow, and take important steps toward building a new legacy—one built on connection and emotional safety.

Your childhood might have left wounds that are difficult to face, but even in that pain, you've found the courage to consider a different path. Parenting while working through your own past isn't always smooth. Some days will feel heavy—old habits might resurface, and doubts may sneak in. But growth isn't about getting everything right. It's about showing up, learning as you go, and giving yourself grace along the way.

Try to see your progress in the little things, not just the big breakthroughs. When you take a breath before responding, offer your child comfort, or set a boundary that feels right—you're moving forward. These moments might seem small, but they slowly create a home where both you and your child can feel safe and supported.

Your efforts are doing more than creating a better life for your child. They're also rewriting your own story. You're showing yourself the kindness, love, and support that may have been missing in your past. When you give yourself grace for mistakes and celebrate your progress, you heal and grow in ways that ripple through your parenting. This isn't just about breaking the cycle—it's about building something new and meaningful in its place.

Some days will go more smoothly than others, and that's completely normal. Raising a child while growing as a person is an ongoing process, with many chances to pause, learn, and try again. Give yourself permission to take those chances when they show up. The very fact that you're here, reading this guide, says a lot about your dedication to creating a better future. That dedication is far more important than any mistake or moment of uncertainty along the way.

Pay attention to the relationship you're building with your child—that's what real progress looks like. Each time they come to you for comfort or share their feelings, it shows the safe, loving bond you're creating. You're not only raising a child; you're helping shape how they see themselves, connect with others, and feel about the world. That's a lasting and meaningful gift.

Thank you for dedicating your time and effort to this guide. Your commitment to reflecting, learning, and growing is truly inspiring. You've already made important strides toward breaking the cycle and building a future full of love, understanding, and emotional safety for yourself and your child.

Keep going, one day, one step, and one choice at a time. You have everything you need to build the legacy you want—a legacy of care, connection, and hope. The work you're doing matters deeply, and it's making a difference in ways that will echo far beyond today.

FAQs

How do I know if I'm repeating patterns from my own childhood in my parenting?

Recognizing patterns starts with self-awareness. Pay attention to moments when you feel triggered, overreact, or act in ways that surprise you. Ask yourself reflective questions like, "Am I parenting from fear or love?" or "Does this reaction feel familiar from my own childhood?" Journaling or talking with a therapist can help uncover these patterns and guide you toward intentional choices.

What's the difference between setting boundaries and being too controlling as a parent?

Boundaries are about creating a safe, respectful environment for both you and your child, while control often stems from fear or a need for power. Healthy boundaries focus on guiding your child with love and consistency, like setting rules for safety or emotional well-being. Control, on the other hand, may stifle your child's independence or individuality. The key is balance—providing structure while allowing room for growth.

How can I stop feeling guilty when I make mistakes as a parent?

Guilt is a natural response, but it doesn't have to define you. Shift your focus from guilt to grace by reminding yourself that mistakes are opportunities to learn and grow. Apologize to your child when needed, model accountability, and celebrate the effort you're putting into breaking old patterns. Remember, your child doesn't need perfection—they need love, connection, and your willingness to try again.

What are some practical ways to reparent my inner child while raising my own child?

Reparenting your inner child involves giving yourself the care and compassion you may have missed growing up. Practice self-soothing techniques like deep breathing or positive affirmations when you feel triggered. Speak kindly to yourself, as you would to your child, and allow yourself to feel emotions without judgment. By nurturing your inner child, you'll find it easier to respond to your own child with patience and empathy.

How can I teach my child emotional intelligence if I'm still learning it myself?

Start small by modeling emotional awareness and regulation. Name your own feelings out loud, like, "I'm feeling frustrated, so I'm going to take a deep breath." Encourage your child to express their emotions and validate their feelings by saying, “It’s okay to feel sad. I’m here.” As you practice these skills together, you’ll both grow in emotional intelligence.

What should I do if my family doesn’t respect the boundaries I’ve set for my child?

Be clear and consistent about your boundaries, and calmly remind family members when they overstep. Use simple, direct language like, “We’ve decided not to discuss this topic,” or “Please respect our parenting choices.” If boundaries continue to be ignored, consider limiting contact or setting consequences, such as ending visits early. Protecting your child’s emotional safety is your priority, even if it means difficult conversations.

How can I measure progress when breaking the cycle of emotional harm?

Progress isn’t about perfection—it’s about small, meaningful changes. Notice moments when you respond with patience instead of reacting, when you validate your child’s feelings, or when you set a boundary with confidence. Reflect on how your relationship with your child feels—are they coming to you for comfort or expressing their emotions more openly? Celebrate these wins, no matter how small, as they show you’re creating a healthier, more loving environment.

References and Helpful Links

Connell, L. (2024, November 11). Narcissistic and family scapegoat recovery. Laura K. Connell. https://www.laurakconnell.com/blog/daughters-narcissistic-mothers

Charlie Health Editorial Team. (2025, April 11). 10 Symptoms of daughters of Narcissistic Mothers. Charlie Health. https://www.charliehealth.com/post/10-symptoms-of-daughters-of-narcissistic-mothers#:~:text=The%20constant%20demand%20for%20attention,to%20feel%20valued%20or%20significant.

Weinstein, T. (2023, December 4). How having a narcissistic parent impacts young adult mental health. Newport Institute. https://www.newportinstitute.com/resources/mental-health/narcissistic-parent/

Narcissism, A. T. (2024, November 15). Two behavior patterns of how narcissistic mothers treat their daughters. Medium. https://medium.com/read-or-die/two-behavior-patterns-narcissistic-mothers-treat-their-daughters-7350213b5f46

RDIconnect, & RDIconnect. (2022, June 10). Am I overparenting or overcompensating? | RDIConnect. RDIconnect | Parent and Professional Training. https://www.rdiconnect.com/am-i-overparenting-or-overcompensating-the-balance-of-special-needs-parenting/

Walter, E. (2025, January 6). Breaking the cycle — healing for adult daughters of narcissistic mothers. Medium. https://esewrites.medium.com/breaking-the-cycle-healing-for-adult-daughters-of-narcissistic-mothers-06f1f65c2673

Taylor. (2024, November 14). Re-Parenting Yourself: healing your inner child while raising your own children. Integrated Behavioral Health. https://www.integratedbhs.com/re-parenting-yourself-healing-your-inner-child/

iMOM. (2024, July 31). 5 Ways Emotional intelligence Can help you as a Mom - IMOM. iMOM. https://www.imom.com/developing-emotional-intelligence-for-moms/

www.ingramcontent.com/pod-product-compliance
Lightning Source LLC
LaVergne TN
LVHW022022200926
848481LV00007B/2489

* 9 7 9 8 3 4 9 5 2 1 9 1 1 *